# PSYCHIC POWERS

G.L. Cronin

Rourke
Educational Media

rourkeeducationalmedia.com

# Before, During, and After Reading Activities

## Before Reading: Building Background Knowledge and Academic Vocabulary

"Before Reading" strategies activate prior knowledge and set a purpose for reading. Before reading a book, it is important to tap into what your child or students already know about the topic. This will help them develop their vocabulary and increase their reading comprehension.

**Questions and activities to build background knowledge:**
1. *Look at the cover of the book. What will this book be about?*
2. *What do you already know about the topic?*
3. *Let's study the Table of Contents. What will you learn about in the book's chapters?*
4. *What would you like to learn about this topic? Do you think you might learn about it from this book? Why or why not?*

### Building Academic Vocabulary
Building academic vocabulary is critical to understanding subject content.
Assist your child or students to gain meaning of the following vocabulary words.
**Content Area Vocabulary**
Read the list. What do these words mean?
- *foretell*
- *intuition*
- *prophesied*
- *retrocognition*
- *séances*
- *therapists*

## During Reading: Writing Component

"During Reading" strategies help to make connections, monitor understanding, generate questions, and stay focused.
1. *While reading, write in your reading journal any questions you have or anything you do not understand.*
2. *After completing each chapter, write a summary of the chapter in your reading journal.*
3. *While reading, make connections with the text and write them in your reading journal.*
   a) *Text to Self – What does this remind me of in my life? What were my feelings when I read this?*
   b) *Text to Text – What does this remind me of in another book I've read? How is this different from other books I've read?*
   c) *Text to World – What does this remind me of in the real world? Have I heard about this before? (News, current events, school, etc....)*

## After Reading: Comprehension and Extension Activity

"After Reading" strategies provide an opportunity to summarize, question, reflect, discuss, and respond to text. After reading the book, work on the following questions with your child or students to check their level of reading comprehension and content mastery.
1. List examples of psychic powers. *(Summarize)*
2. Why is it difficult to prove psychic powers are real? *(Infer)*
3. What professions might use psychic powers? *(Asking Questions)*
4. Do you know of a situation in which an animal seemed to predict the future? What value could these abilities in animals have to humans? *(Text to Self Connection)*

**Extension Activity**
Which topic that you read about most interests you? Research the topic using reliable sources. What did you discover? Craft a story, play, or poem about characters using psychic powers.

# Table of Contents

Extrasensory Perception ..................... 4

Dream a Little Dream ..................... 14

Prophecies and Predictions .............. 18

Psychics at Work ..................... 24

Memory Game ..................... 30

Index ..................... 31

Show What You Know ..................... 31

Further Reading ..................... 31

About the Author ..................... 32

# Extrasensory Perception

Many people believe in psychic powers. Others credit luck. What do you think? Extrasensory perception (ESP) uses abilities beyond the five senses of sight, smell, hearing, taste, and touch.

Starting in the 1880s, some
theater acts often included
mind-reading demonstrations.

France

Think of telepathy as a way for the brain to send mind messages to others. With telepathy, individuals communicate through thoughts.

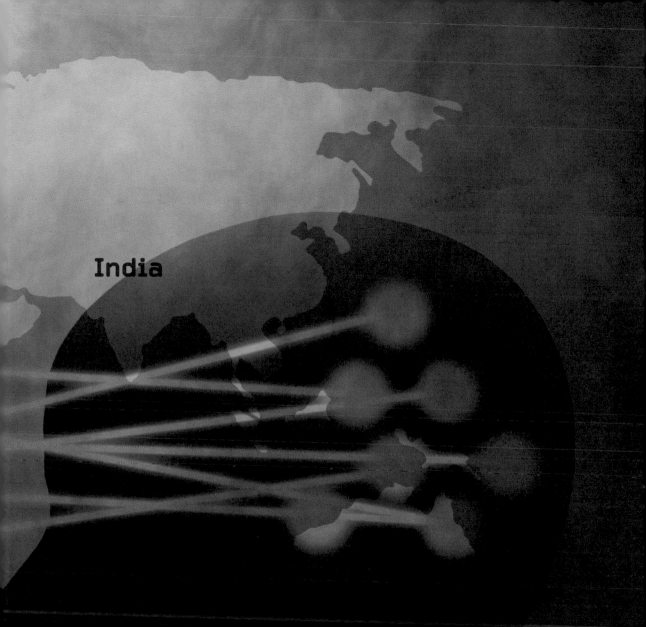

India

Harvard University researchers led successful brain-to-brain experiments. Using flashes of light, subjects sent brain communications from India to France.

Joan of Arc claimed she was visited by Saint Michael the Archangel, shown here in a painting by Eugène Thirion.

Clairvoyants claim to view pictures of the future. From age 13, Joan of Arc's visions inspired her actions. At age 18, she led the French army. Her army defeated the English.

*Joan of Arc never fought in a battle. She rode alongside her men holding a banner instead of a weapon.*

Psychokinesis moves objects using only the mind's energy, not by physical touch. Some slot-machine players say psychokinesis lets them win!

## ESP on TV

The *Charmed* reboot features a psychokinetic character, Macy.

Do previous lives exist? Psychics use **retrocognition** to peek into the past. Often, these psychics hold objects from history. They claim this strengthens psychic energy.

 **retrocognition** (RE-tro-kahg-ni-shuhn  n): the ability to see a past time period

# Mind Games

Developers are working on a video game controlled by players' brainwaves.

Dream a Little Dream

Most precognition occurs during dreams.
Abraham Lincoln woke from a disturbing dream
before being assassinated. Did Abraham's dream
**foretell** his own death?

 **foretell** (for-TELL): to know something in advance

Medium Theresa Caputo claims dead relatives' spirits may appear within dreams. Why? They reassure dreamers.

# Chasing Dreams

Do your dreams include eggs or newspapers? Expect good luck! No surprise, lava-spewing volcanoes predict bad luck. Many dreamers experience "chase" nightmares. These common nightmares reflect daytime worries.

# Prophecies and Predictions

Nostradamus

Before working as a 16th century seer, Nostradamus became a doctor and studied astrology. He later scribbled his predictions within his poetry. Believers claim he **prophesied** World Wars I and II, and Adolph Hitler's birth.

**prophesied** (PRA-fih-seed): told of the future

Edgar Cayce predicted the Great Depression. Edgar urged his friends to leave the stock market. He said the Great Depression would occur in 1929. It did.

THE SLEEPING PROPHET

EDGAR CAYCE (1877-1945), was internationally accepted as an extremely gifted psychic. An humble man, he never profited materially from his psychic ability, but used it to help "make manifest the love of God and man." Operated his photography studio and lived in this building from 1912 until 1923. Many psychic readings were given here during that time.

During a live radio show in 1995, Tana Hoy foresaw an upcoming major bombing. The Oklahoma City bombing occurred 90 minutes later.

## Animals on Alert

Do animals have a sixth sense? Six days before Japan's 2011 earthquake, residents said cats acted strangely. Farmers noted cows produced less milk. In some cultures, people believe a howling dog warns of an upcoming death.

# Psychics at Work

The Fox sisters, from left to right: Margaret, Kate, and Leah

Mediums chat with the dead. In 1848, the Fox sisters of New York became famous mediums. They performed **séances**. Authorities later exposed the Fox sisters as frauds.

# The Sleeping Prophet

The "Sleeping Prophet" worked as a psychic doctor. To diagnose, Edgar Cayce snoozed. Once awakened, he gave medical advice. His psychic work landed him in jail twice.

**séances** (SAY-ans-is): group attempts to contact and communicate with the dead

Some people now seek psychic therapists rather than standard treatment. These **therapists** read clients' energy. Psychic therapists offer life suggestions.

**therapists** (THE-re-pihsts): individuals who help others who experience emotional concerns

# Scene of the Crime

Crime victims' families sometimes believe psychic detectives can provide valuable clues. Thirty-five percent of urban police departments accept psychics' help.

Mentalists listen. They observe details and people's behavior. Mentalists such as Derren Brown amaze audiences. Does he read minds? No. Mentalists use **intuition**.

**intuition** (IN-too-i-shuhn): the ability to know something through a gut feeling

James Randi

# The Skeptics' Side

Many Americans believe psychic powers exist. Skeptics disagree. James Randi, a former magician, offered a million dollars to anyone whose psychic abilities could be proven. In 2015, the challenge ended. No one collected the prize.

# Memory Game

Can you match the image to what you read?

# Index

Brown, Derren 28

Cayce, Edgar  20, 25

clairvoyants 9

Lincoln, Abraham 15

medium(s) 16, 24

mentalists 28

psychic(s) 12, 24, 25, 26, 27, 29

psychic detectives 27

psychokinesis 10

Sleeping Prophet 25

telepathy  6

# Show What You Know

1. What is psychokinesis?

2. What is a skeptic?

3. What country is Joan of Arc from?

4. What does it mean if you experience the common nightmare of being chased?

5. How did Nostradamus reveal his psychic predictions?

# Further Reading

Kelly, Erin Entrada, *Hello, Universe*, Green Willow Books, 2017.

Noll, Elizabeth, *ESP*, Black Rabbit Books, 2017.

Seeley, M.H., *Freaky Stories about the Paranormal*, Gareth Stevens Publishing, 2016.

# About the Author

G.L. Cronin enjoys researching intriguing topics. In addition to writing, she works as a middle school librarian.

*Photo by Teresa Cronin*

**Meet The Author!**
www.meetREMauthors.com

www.rourkeeducationalmedia.com

PHOTO CREDITS: Cover and Title Pg ©Selimaksan; Pg 12, 15, 18, 26, 28 ©LueratSatichob; Pg 3-32 ©aldra; Pg 12 & 30 ©jinjo0222988; Pg 16 & 30 ©D-Keine; Pg 21 & 30 ©ImagineGolf; Pg 6 & 30 ©123ducu; Pg 8 & 30 ©Wiki; Pg 14 & 30 ©ilbusca; Pg 11, 13, 17, 22, 25, 27, 29 ©ulimi; Pg 3 ©teekid; Pg 4 ©TSchon; Pg 5 ©Library of Congress; Pg 6 ©lukbar; Pg 9 ©Jef Wodniack; Pg 10 ©skynesher; Pg 11 ©Bet_Noire; Pg 13 ©gremlin; Pg 15 ©PPRE2A-00088; Pg 17 ©RomoloTavani; Pg 18 ©imagentix, ©Wiki; Pg 19 ©icholakov, ©Hoffmann, Heinrich wiki; Pg 20 ©Wiki; Pg 21 ©DNY59; Pg 22 ©GlobalP; Pg 23 ©Staff Sgt. Preston Chasteen, Pg 24 ©Wiki; Pg 25 ©Renphoto; Pg 26 ©KatarzynaBialasiewicz; Pg 27 ©Kutsuks; Pg 28 ©Django; Pg 29 ©Wiki, ©NosUA

Edited by: Keli Sipperley
Cover and interior design by: Kathy Walsh

**Library of Congress PCN Data**

Psychic Powers / G.L. Cronin
 (Unexplained)
 ISBN 978-1-64369-035-3 (hard cover)
 ISBN 978-1-64369-103-9 (soft cover)
 ISBN 978-1-64369-182-4 (e-Book)
Library of Congress Control Number: 2018956020

Rourke Educational Media
Printed in the United States of America,
North Mankato, Minnesota